beautiful ribbons

beautiful ribbons

mary norden

photography by sandra lane

RUNNING PRESS

Philadelphia • London

Library of Congress Cataloging-in-
Publication number 98-66880

ISBN 0-7624-0362-4

Printed and bound in China

This edition published in the
United States in 1999 by
Running Press Book Publishers
125 South Twenty-second Street
Philadelphia, Pennsylvania
19103-4399

Visit us on the web!
www.runningpress.com

Publishing Director Anne Ryland

Designer Sally Powell

Editor Jo Lethaby

Editorial Manager
Sian Parkhouse

Production Alison Jones

Stylist Mary Norden

Additional photography

David Murray: 20, 40, 50, 58, 66,
88, 98, 132, 142–151
Jonathan Lovekin: 16–17, 117

introduction 6

ribbons in the home 10
bed linen and blankets 14
ribbon border bed cover 20
curtains 30
tiebacks 36
ruffled ribbon pillow 40
pillows and bolsters 44
ribbon-weave pillow 50
lampshades 54
ribbon-bound lampshade 58
photo frames and pictures 62
tassels 66
napkins, mats, and tablecloths 70

ribbons for festive occasions 80
finishing touches 84
ribbon roses 88
tables and chairs 94
wreath bows 98
celebration cakes 104
special presentation 106
festive decorations 116
ribbon wreaths 122

ribbons and flowers 126
posies 130
ribbon-wrapped bouquet 132
boutonnieres 136
vases and flowerpots 140

types of ribbon 142
tying bows 146
acknowledgments and suppliers 151

Most people traditionally associate ribbons only with gifts and bunches of flowers, but the almost overwhelming choice of ribbons now available means that it is possible to find one for every need, occasion, and taste. The inspirational ideas and numerous projects in this book make use of a wide variety of different ribbon types, but by no means all, as well as showing the versatility of ribbon, which goes far beyond decorating Christmas presents and wedding bouquets.

The book is divided into three main creative sections, *Ribbons in the Home*, *Ribbons for Festive Occasions,* and *Ribbons and Flowers*. The book finishes with a technical section, which includes a directory on types of ribbons used and step-by-step instructions on tying the different bows found throughout the book.

The first and largest section of the book illustrates the use of ribbons in the home—from enhancing soft furnishings and trimming bed and table linen to hanging and decorating pictures and mirrors. Any projects that involve sewing are kept very simple, requiring only the most basic of stitching, which can often be achieved without the use of a sewing machine, although it might take a little longer. Projects such as embellishing lampshades need no more than glue, and others such as curtain tiebacks and some blankets, for example, require no additional materials—simply an attractive length of ribbon tied around or threaded through the fabric and finished with an exquisite bow.

The second section is full of ideas for making a festive occasion even more special by adding a touch of individual style. From original presentation of gifts and food to finishing touches for the table and decorating furniture and entire rooms, the ideas are certainly not intended only for Christmas, but include any number of special events or celebrations

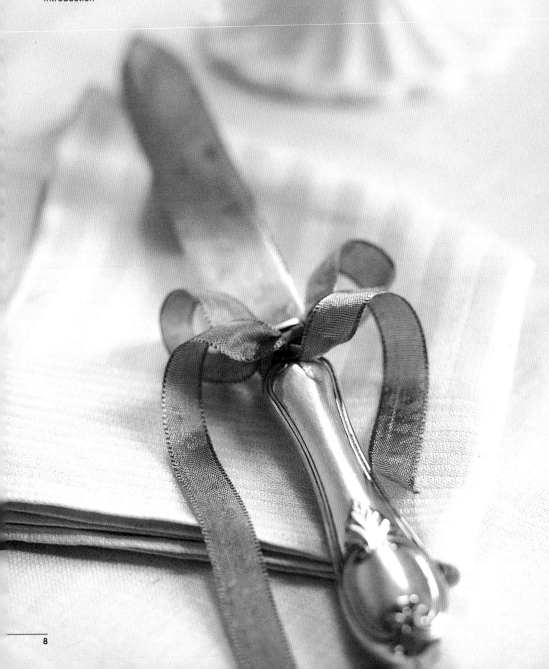

throughout the year—a spring wedding or a summer garden party, dinner parties, birthdays, and anniversaries. Ideas can easily be adapted to suit any occasion simply by changing the type of ribbon or its color. For example, a table decorated with brightly colored polka-dot ribbons is more suited to an alfresco meal, but for a winter dinner party by candlelight, lengths of plaid ribbon would be more in keeping—especially for New Year's Eve or Burns Night. The success of all of these festive ideas, as with those in the rest of the book, depends on keeping it simple. A napkin rolled and tied with a plain bow has far more impact than one that is smothered in a complicated mass of ribbon; likewise, one single-colored bow on the back of a chair with long tails that fall and flutter down towards the seat is far more effective than several stiff multicolored bows.

The third section of the book reinforces the pleasure of using ribbons with flowers— from the tiniest boutonnieres and posies to ribbon-wrapped bouquets and vases and flowerpots. A bunch of flowers casually picked during an amble around the backyard can be transformed into the realms of chic with the right bow. Similarly, a little foliage from a hedge decorated with an interesting ribbon makes a far more striking and individual corsage than the traditional and rather predictable rosebud or carnation.

The aim of this book is not only to show how versatile and effective ribbons can be, but also to inspire you, the reader, to create your own ideas and ways of using the many wonderful types of ribbon available.

Mary Norden

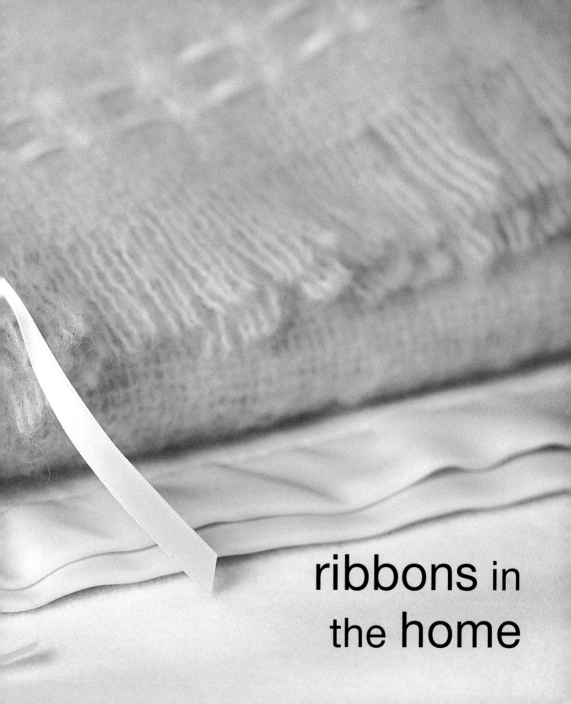

ribbons in
the home

Ribbons offer an easy way of adding style to your home, whether your theme is modern or traditional. Their most obvious use is with soft furnishings. Add single lengths of ribbon to the edges of curtains and to plain bed and table linen to make striking borders. Use ribbons tied into decorative bows to close pillowcases and scatter-cushion covers instead of zippers or buttons, or use a length of ribbon to tie back a curtain.

Other ideas for using ribbon around the home include using it to hang pictures and mirrors and to trim lampshades, shelf and table edges; and add a ribbon border to personalize a glass clip frame. Use ribbons to coordinate interiors, too: for example, in a living room use the same ribbon to trim the edge of a plain linen curtain and to trim the lampshade; in a pretty bedroom, use it to decorate the bed linen and as a curtain tieback. As always, the possibilities are virtually endless.

bed linen
and blankets

There are many different ways of using ribbon to decorate bed linen and blankets, and with different results. For example, crisp white bed linen trimmed with straight lines of navy ribbon looks chic and dramatically different from that decorated with gathered and ruffled ribbons in soft feminine colors. For children there are pictorial ribbons with simple images of teddy bears, dolls, and boats. Ribbons on bed linen can have practical uses, too. Ribbon ties, for example, can be used instead of buttons to fasten the openings of pillowcases and duvet covers.

For trimming bed linen you need a ribbon that is both washable and colorfast, while for decorating blankets, delicate ribbons that require dry cleaning, such as velvets, grosgrains, and intricate jacquards woven with metallic

above right Plain and striped lilac ribbons are used to decorate three different pillowcases, which look lovely when mixed together on this wrought-iron bed.

below right A pretty sprigged pillowcase is edged with two rows of purple satin ribbon. Each length of ribbon is sewn on with just one row of stitching in matching thread.

far right The opening of a seersucker pillowcase is closed with pairs of lilac ribbon tied into bows. The ribbon was originally a wire-edge ribbon, but the wire was removed prior to sewing.

threads can also be used. Most woven-edge, and a few wire-edge, ribbons are washable—the wire in the latter needs removing by gentle pulling before using it for bed linen.

To secure the ribbon, stitch along each side of it as close to the edge as possible or, for very narrow ribbon, one row of stitching along the center is adequate. Alternatively, give the ribbon a slightly ruffled effect (see page 40) before sewing it on in a straight or wavy line.

If you are making your own bed linen and blankets, the ribbon ends can be incorporated into the seam or hem allowances; otherwise, you need to tuck under the raw ends before sewing the ribbon in place.

above left A pillowcase is closed with taffeta ribbon tied into bows.
below left An exquisite braid of tiny flowers made of folded ombré ribbon is secured with hand stitching along the opening edge of a pillowcase.
right Three pillows demonstrate different decorative options.

far left A pile of pressed plain sheets edged with ribbon demonstrates the use of various hard-wearing pictorial jacquard ribbons—a wonderful option for children's bed linen.

left A cotton jacquard ribbon woven with roses and edged with pink easily transforms a plain white sheet into pretty, feminine bed linen.

above The same sheet looks even more romantic when used on an old French day bed. The Oxford pillow-case is trimmed with red rickrack the same color as the jacquard roses.

ribbon border bed cover

To make the lattice border for the 76 inches long bed cover shown here,

you will need 4½ yards of ⅜ inch-wide cotton ribbon in red and 3¾ yards of

checked ribbon in the same width for each border.

one   Mark the position of the red ribbon on the bed cover using a tape measure

and pins. Position the two rows 2 inches apart, with the first row 4 inches from the

bottom edge of the cover. In each row place the first and the final pins about ¾ inches in

from the side edges of the cover, with the other pins at 5¾ inch intervals in between. Fold under the first ⅜ inch of the

ribbon to hide the raw edge and pin the end onto the cover at the first pin. Measure

6 inches of ribbon and pin this to the cover at the second pin position. Repeat this pro-

cess across the cover and for both rows of the border. Finish each row with the ribbon

ends turned under, as at the beginning of the row. The extra ribbon between each pair

of pins allows the two rows to be tied together without

distorting the cover.   **two**   Machine-stitch or handsew

the ribbon to the cover only at the points where the pins are positioned.   **three**   Cut the

checked ribbon into lengths of 10 inches. Slide these under the two rows of red ribbon,

positioning one halfway between each set of stitching; tie each checked length into a

simple bow, pulling the two rows of red ribbon together.

Extra-wide satin ribbon is the traditional choice for hemming blankets. An alternative, however, is to use the narrowest satin ribbon and, using a blunt-ended tapestry or darning needle, thread it through loosely woven blanket fabric, such as mohair, to make border patterns. Choose ribbon no wider than ⅜ inch; otherwise, it will distort both the ribbon and the blanket, and use a double-face ribbon if the ends are to be tied in a bow.

left Two cream blankets, one mohair, the other plain wool, are trimmed in different ways with satin ribbon. The narrower ribbon is laced through the loosely woven fabric while the wider ribbon is sewn on to form a satin hem.
right Two rows of narrow satin ribbon have been laced through the blanket and the ribbon ends secured with a knot and a bow at both ends of the laced border. The type of ribbon used affects whether the ribbon ends are secured with small and neat simple bows, which may be stitched down, or with the lengthier and looser bows shown here.

right A fine silk jacquard ribbon with a delicate paisley pattern in shades of gray adds a touch of luxury to an otherwise plain blanket. The blanket was made from a length of wide woolen fabric, and the ribbon was sewn along only one side of the blanket. The other blanket is made from thicker wool and decorated with a narrow floral jacquard ribbon in black and beige.

far right Two Oxford pillowcases are finished with a stylish edging of ribbon. The wavy rickrack ribbon contrasts with the striped fabric of one pillowcase, and the checked ribbon in black and beige adds pattern to the other plain pillowcase. Both of these ribbons are made of cotton and are hardwearing, which makes them an ideal choice to use on bed linen.

right and far right A Chinese silk curtain is hung from a metal pole with lengths of satin ribbon. Each ribbon tie was evenly spaced along the top edge of the curtain and stitched in place before being threaded through a curtain ring and tied in a bow.

above A plain cream curtain has been given a stripy decorative finishing touch with vertical rows of narrow ribbon threaded through the loosely woven curtain fabric.

curtains

Just as everyday bed linen can be turned into something special and individual with a length of ribbon and a few stitches so, too, can curtains. Since continual washing and general wear and tear is not such a consideration when choosing ribbons for curtains as it is for bed linen, the choice of ribbon type and the way in which it can be applied to a curtain is even greater—pleated satin, silk velvet, jacquard, and picot-edge organdy can now all be used. Again, ribbons on curtains can be functional as well as decorative, and one of the prettiest ways by which to hang a curtain is with lengths of ribbon tied into bows or even just simply knotted. The ribbon ends can either be trimmed short or left long so that they fall in with the folds of the curtain.

The curtain fabric and how you wish to decorate it will influence the choice of ribbon, particularly if a lot of sewing is involved. For example, if a long length of ribbon is to be sewn flat along the edge of a curtain to form a decorative border or hem, it must be made of a suitable fabric. A jacquard or a satin ribbon would be appropriate for a velvet curtain because the fabrics are of a similar weight. A sheer ribbon, however, would be too delicate and would pucker during sewing.

Ribbon can be sewn in a single length along the edge of a curtain to form a border, or several lengths can be arranged horizontally or vertically across the curtain fabric for a striped effect. If the fabric is loosely woven, you could try weaving narrow ribbon through the fabric with a blunt-ended needle, as with the blankets earlier. Other patterns can be made by applying ribbon not as lengths but as ready-made single bows, which can be arranged in rows along one edge or scattered randomly across the curtain. Sew each bow into position by hand with a few backstitches. With fine curtain fabric, such as organdy or voile, leave the tails long so they flutter like butterflies when the window is open and the curtain moves in the breeze.

Alternative "curtains" for windows and doors can be made simply by hanging lengths of ribbon. Use one

left and far left Lengths of rayon ribbon in pretty shades of pink, beige, silver gray, and tan are tied into bows and then placed randomly across a fine cotton curtain. They are secured in position with a few hand stitches.

single type of ribbon, or try an assortment in complementary colors, varying the length and width of the ribbons for extra interest. Tie or staple one end of each ribbon length to a wooden curtain pole and tie the other end to interesting objects such as glass baubles, or thread the end through shells, making holes if necessary with a hand drill. Different ribbon textures create different types of curtain: lengths of sheer ribbon will produce a romantic ethereal curtain as opposed to the more solid effect achieved with thicker nontranslucent ribbon.

above, left and right A window is decorated with sea shells hung from pieces of ribbon in a pretty assortment of aqua colors and of various widths and lengths. A mixture of ribbon types has also been used—plain and shot organdy, cotton, and rayon.

left As an alternative to a shell and ribbon "curtain," glass balls are tied and hung in the same way. For this window dressing, sheer ribbons only have been used, and a simple bow in another ribbon in a complementary color has been added to the top of each ball.

tiebacks

Tiebacks are usually crescent shaped and made of fabric that matches or contrasts with the curtain fabric. Although very neat, they often appear rather stiff, and you might prefer instead to hold curtains back with casually tied lengths of ribbon. For this look to work you cannot be sparing with the ribbon—use plenty of it so that after tying, the long ends can drape down among the curtain folds. A velvet curtain loosely tied back with a wide pleated ribbon looks wonderfully sumptuous like this,

and the ribbon has a habit of twisting gently as it falls. Alternatively, the ribbon can be tied into a bow. If you choose to use a sheer ribbon for a tieback, give the bow more substance and interest by mixing two different but complementary sheer ribbons.

The type of ribbon and tieback is influenced by the style of the room and the curtain fabric. A kitchen curtain made from blue and white striped ticking looks best tied back with a simple plain blue cotton ribbon. A luxurious ribbon such as velvet or satin, or a complicated bow would be the wrong choice for both the room and the type of fabric. In contrast, a romantic bedroom window dressed with a voile or organdy curtain looks wonderfully ethereal tied back with another sheer—look for exquisite appliquéd organdy and satin-edge georgette. On the other hand, a living room with vibrant colored curtains would need something stronger, such as a wide striped ribbon in fluorescent colors or a print. Some of the best brightly colored or patterned wide ribbons are wire-edge ribbons. These ribbons are ideal for molding into elaborate bows and will hold their shape indefinitely, but if you prefer your tieback to be more relaxed and floppy, simply remove the wire from the ribbon.

To make your tieback more elaborate, you could add a ribbon tassel (see page 66) or an extra bow to the first length of ribbon, or even a rosette bow (see page 150).

far left Ribbons offer an almost effortless way of tying back a curtain, particularly since there is little or no sewing involved. Here, a wide pleated taffeta ribbon with a wire edge, "shot" with fluorescent pink and orange, is tied casually to hold back a pink organdy curtain.

left A short length of old checked taffeta ribbon found in a thrift shop was not quite long enough to make a tieback, so it was stitched on top of another slightly wider and much longer single-colored taffeta ribbon. The finished ribbon was wrapped twice around the curtain before being tied into a bow, so that the checked pattern is clearly visible.

A printed voile curtain is pulled back with a wonderfully frothy bow
of polka-dot organdy ribbon. The ribbon has been wrapped around the
curtain and tied into a classic bow, then another bow tied directly on
top of the first one to form a type of double bow.

ruffled ribbon pillow

To calculate the amount of ribbon required for each ruffled stripe, measure the length of the chosen

pillow cover fabric and multiply by 1½ to include gathering the ribbon and a seam allowance. For

a fuller ruffle allow more ribbon per stripe. For the total amount of ribbon required for each pillow,

multiply this calculation by the number of stripes. When choosing your ribbon, avoid thicker ribbon

types such as velvet and grosgrain. The pale pink ribbon used here is 1½ inches wide.

one Fold each length of ribbon in half lengthwise

and press lightly. This creates a crease, which marks

the center of the ribbon. Run a gathering thread in a

contrasting color along this crease either by hand or

machine. Carefully gather the ribbon by pulling one end of thread. If you have used a sewing machine, pull the spool

thread. **two** When the ribbon is ruffled to the required length, allowing a little extra for a seam allowance within

the pillow cover, secure the thread ends with a knot or backstitches. Distribute the ruffles evenly down the length of the

ribbon, then pin it in position on the fabric as shown.

Using matching thread sew the ribbon onto the fabric

with a line of machine or hand stitching worked as close

as possible to the gathering line. Finally, unpick the

contrasting colored line of gathering stitches.

pillows
and bolsters

There are numerous ways in which ribbon can be used
to turn a bland pillow or bolster that fades into the back-
ground into something special that gets noticed. One way
is to apply ribbon as a border to emphasize the outline of
the pillow. Simple ribbon trims can be added by hand to
an existing cover, while more flamboyant frills need to be
incorporated into the seams when assembling a pillow
cover. Another technique is to use ribbons to create
geometric patterns on an otherwise plain fabric—grids,
stripes, and diagonals are all possibilities. Mix different
widths of ribbon as well as different patterns, but keep to
the same type of ribbon texture. The ribbons can either
be applied flat with one or two rows of machine stitching,
or ruffled first and then sewn on to give a frilled effect
across the pillow cover (see page 40). Lengths of
ribbon of equal length can also be interwoven to create a
striking pillow cover (see page 50). If you are weaving
ribbon, use several colors for a checkerboard effect or
just one color to show off the weave better.

above right White seersucker has been decorated with
lengths of narrow blue and white gingham ribbon before
being made into a pillow cover. Sewn along one long edge
only, the ribbon gently ripples over the fabric.
right and far right Various blue and white ribbons are
sewn onto pillow covers in bold geometric patterns.

More ribbon ideas for cushions: a linen slip
cover is closed with ties of checked ribbon and
a narrow ruffled ribbon acts as a border.

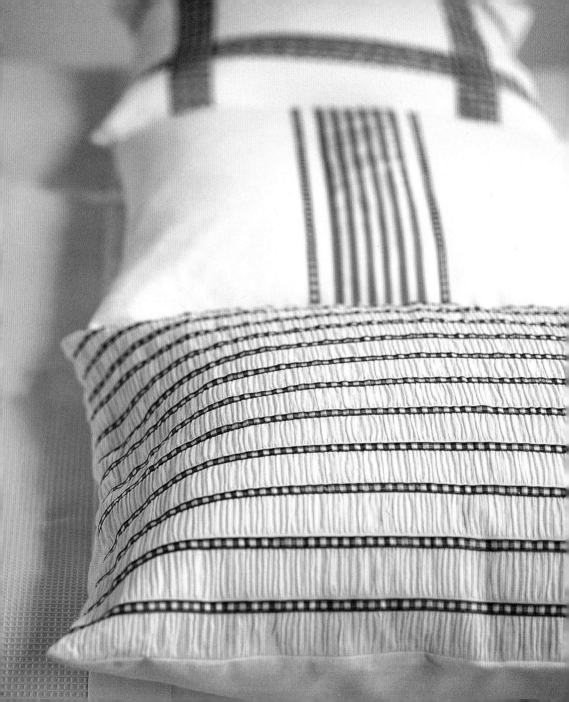

Ribbons also make effective fastenings, and ribbon ties are simpler than inserting zippers or sewing on buttons for closing a pillow or bolster cover. Bolsters in particular have a tendency to look very formal and tailored, so using ribbon to close the ends gives a softer, more relaxed feel as well as reducing the amount of sewing necessary.

left An exquisite iridescent moiré ribbon with dotted edges is tied into simple bows to fasten each end of a silk bolster.

right A ruffled double border made by layering satin and organdy ribbon adds an extra touch of luxury to a Chinese silk pillow. The two ribbons were basted and then gathered together along one edge to the required length, then incorporated into the assembling of the cover.

below The front opening of a pillow is closed with a pair of satin ribbons tied in a floppy bow.

ribbon-weave pillow

The amount of ribbon required is determined by the ribbon width and the area to be covered. To make this 14 inch square ribbon-weave pillow front, you will need 7½ yards of 1½ inch wide ribbon, plus a 15 inch square of cotton fabric.

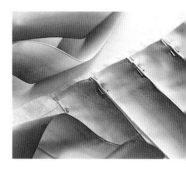

one Mark the pillow's ½ inch seam allowance on the four edges of the fabric, using a washable fabric marker. Cut the ribbon into 18 lengths of 15 inches. Pin half of the strips along one edge of the fabric, making sure the ends are within the seam allowance and that there is no gap between the strips. Machine stitch within ½ inch of the edge of the fabric. Repeat along the opposite edge to secure the ribbons. **two** Place the remaining strips over the secured ribbons at right angles, butting the first strip against the top row of stitching and the last strip against the bottom row of stitching. Pin, then sew along one edge only, again within the pillow's seam allowance, close to the first secured strip, but taking care not to catch it in the stitching. **three** Take the unstitched

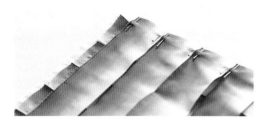

ribbon ends and weave them alternately under and over the lower ribbons. Machine stitch to secure, as before.

Make into a pillow cover.

l i f t   f l a p ▶

lampshades

below left A plain lampshade has been decorated with lengths of a narrow picot-edge ombré ribbon arranged in stripes. Each stripe was glued in position, then finished with a tiny bow along the bottom edge. A clothespin was used to hold the bows in place until the glue was dry.

below right Lengths of rayon ribbon give this lampshade its striped effect. Once the rayon was glued in place, a wired braid ribbon was attached to the top and bottom to finish off the edges and add an extra decorative touch.

right A plain lampshade was punched with holes through which an iridescent grosgrain ribbon was threaded and its ends secured with a bow.

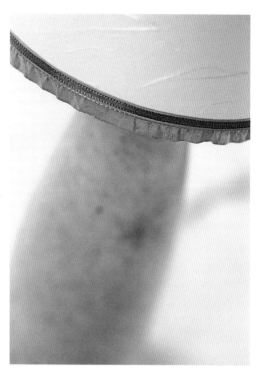

far left A striped lampshade with a twist: evenly spaced lengths of grosgrain ribbon were glued along the inside top edge of the shade. Once well stuck, the ribbon was twisted twice before being glued in position at the other end.

center A cone-shaped lampshade is decorated with alternating stripes of rickrack and grosgrain in shades of lime green, turquoise, and lilac for a fresh, contemporary look.

left Braid made of tiny colored circles of coiled wired yarn is wound decoratively around a plain lampshade.

above A ruffle-edge taffeta ribbon in a contrasting color finishes the edges of another lampshade.

ribbon-bound lampshade

The size of the shade and the degree to which it slopes determine the amount of ribbon required.

For a rough calculation, wind a length of string around one-quarter of the frame. Space it along the

bottom ring slightly closer than the width of the ribbon to be used, and even closer together along

the top ring to allow for overlap and the slope of the shade (unless it is

straight). For the total amount of ribbon required, multiply the length of

string used by four, adding an extra 2 inches for starting and finishing.

one Starting inside the bottom ring of the frame, fold 1 inch of one ribbon end over and

around the ring. Stick firmly in place with a little multipurpose glue. If necessary, secure

with a clothespin until the glue is dry. **two** With the ribbon facing out and

kept taut, bring it up the outside of the frame, over the top ring and back down

inside to overlap the start slightly. Continue wrapping this way tightly. The rib-

bon will need to overlap slightly more at the top

of the shade than at the bottom to account for

any slope. If you run out of ribbon, neatly glue or stitch a second length to the first, inside

the shade near the bottom or top. **three** When the frame is covered, secure the ribbon

end with glue on the inside, or on the outside at the bottom if it will be covered by braid.

Glue braid in position and secure with clothespins until dry.

l i f t f l a p ▶

photo frames and pictures

Decorating plain photo frames with lengths of ribbon is a far more innovative and creative option than simply slipping the picture into a ready-made frame. Unless the glass needs to be cut specially to fit the picture, inexpensive clip frames are ideal for using in this way.

If necessary, first cover the mat with paper—off-white or cream is better than brilliant white paper and, if possible, use paper that has some texture. Position the picture on the mat and secure it in place with a little multipurpose glue or double-sided tape. Place the glass on top and bind the edges of the mat and glass together with masking tape, making sure the tape overlaps the front of the

frame by less than the width of the ribbon to be used. Cut four strips of ribbon to fit the edges of the frame, allowing a little extra for wrapping over the frame edge to the back. Keeping the ribbon taut, anchor the strips along the top and bottom edges first, before positioning the two remaining strips on the sides. For small pictures, a dab of glue at each corner, front and back, is usually enough. For larger pictures a little glue along the edges of the strips of ribbon will be necessary, but be careful not to apply too much glue; otherwise, you might spoil the ribbon. It is best to test the ribbon beforehand to see how well it will take the glue. Hold the ribbon in place with a clothespin until the glue is dry.

Hard-wearing grosgrain ribbon is ideal for covering shades, and different effects are possible with ombré ribbon, which gradually shades from dark to light, according to whether you overlap the dark or the paler edge as you wind it around the lampshade.

left and far left A group of family photographs is framed with different but coordinating ribbons—a suede ribbon, a striped ribbon made of paper, and a wider striped satin sheer, all in sophisticated shades of brown. For framing pictures choose suitable ribbons such as grosgrain, woven jacquard, and satin, which have more stability and strength than delicate single sheers. Not only are sheers too fragile on their own, but their translucent quality is completely lost when glued down.

right A collection of old postcards is grouped together vertically, running down a length of blue satin ribbon, which is cut into an inverted 'V' shape at the bottom and finished at the top with a floppy bow.

left Larger pictures and mirrors, like this one framed in painted bamboo, look good hung with ribbon, especially if you want to make more of a feature of them. If they are very heavy, hang them with wire or string, then hide the wire with a long length of ribbon, such as the wide lilac satin used here, and finish the ribbon with a simple bow.

below A group of botanical prints are hung individually from lengths of gold iridescent grosgrain and arranged along the wall in a row.

Hanging cards with ribbon is usually something done only at Christmas, which is a shame since it is a wonderful way of displaying pictures and photographs that might otherwise be left in a drawer or a pile. Using ribbon this way also means you can decorate your home with an interesting and personal touch. The arrangement of pictures can either be horizontal, in which case each picture is hung from its own length of ribbon, or in a long vertical row with all the pictures on the same ribbon. Secure your pictures to the ribbon with double-sided tape and attach the top of the ribbon to the wall with a picture pin or small nail, which can then be concealed by a small bow.

tassels

Tassels are incredibly easy and quick to make. Almost any type of narrow ribbon can be used. The length of the tassel depends on the size of the piece of cardboard used, and its thickness on the number of times you wind the ribbon around it—the more ribbon you use, the fuller the tassel will be.

For the tassel shown here, you need about 2¾ yards of ⅛ inch wide satin ribbon, plus 10 inches of slightly wider ribbon in a contrasting color for attaching the tassel to the key.

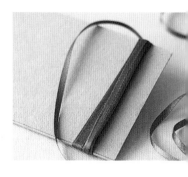

one Cut a piece of cardboard 3 inches wide. Holding one end of the ribbon against the card to begin, wind all of the ribbon around the card. Do not let the ribbon twist. **two** Slip the length of contrasting ribbon under all the strands on the cardboard and knot it firmly at the top of the cardboard as shown, leaving the ends long. These ends are used to tie the tassel to the key.

three Slide the tassel off the cardboard. Wind a small length of satin ribbon (in a matching or a contrasting color) around the tassel, about ⅜ inch from the top; knot firmly. Trim the ends and tuck them underneath or secure with a few stitches.

napkins, mats, and tablecloths

For decorating table linen, always select the ribbons with care. Consider how the linen is going to be used and how often. For example, a napkin or tablecloth that might be used on a regular basis should be trimmed with a hard-wearing washable ribbon such as checked cotton or rickrack, while a delicate napkin made of voile and used only for special occasions could be decorated with something more dainty, like an intricately worked braid or narrow jacquard ribbon.

Ribbon tassels add opulence to curtain tiebacks, table corners, the backs of bridal chairs, and even door handles, while tiny tassels can be tied to keys, gifts, and rolled napkins as a finishing touch.

far left A narrow grosgrain ribbon edged with running stitches in cream adds interest to a plain maroon napkin and gives it style.

center left top Delicate braid enlivens the edges of a cotton napkin.

center left bottom A braided ribbon has been handsewn onto a translucent voile napkin in a diagonal cross, using tiny running stitches and the occasional backstitch.

left For a neat finish on this linen napkin with a frayed edge, the ribbon trim has been folded into a diagonal pleat at each corner before sewing.

A cheerful mix of table mats trimmed
with one or two rows of rickrack,
together with a napkin tied with ribbon
in complementary bright sunny colors,
looks effective on a white tablecloth.

For sets of coordinated table linen, try using the same patterned ribbon in different widths: trim a tablecloth with a wide checked ribbon and the napkins with a narrower version. Alternatively, a narrow ribbon on a napkin or mat could be applied in several rows along a tablecloth to look like a wide ribbon border.

Experiment with different ways of arranging the ribbon, too. Appliqué two lengths of ribbon across table linen, either diagonally or horizontally and vertically, to form a striking cross. Place two or three rows of ribbon on each side of a table mat rather than all the way around. Or try layering ribbons—rickrack on top of a wider ribbon with straight edges, for example—and if the linen has a drawn threadwork border, lace narrow ribbon through the fabric.

right A red grosgrain ribbon embroidered with cream contrasts smartly with a blue jute table mat. **far right** Trim a set of mats with different but coordinating ribbons rather than have them all identical.

Two different ribbons, a plain cotton and a narrow
ombré with a picot edge, have been appliquéd
onto a pale blue tablecloth in a simple grid
pattern. To complement the tablecloth, surplus
ribbon is tied together into a bow around the
neck of a small glass vase.

ribbons for
festive occasions

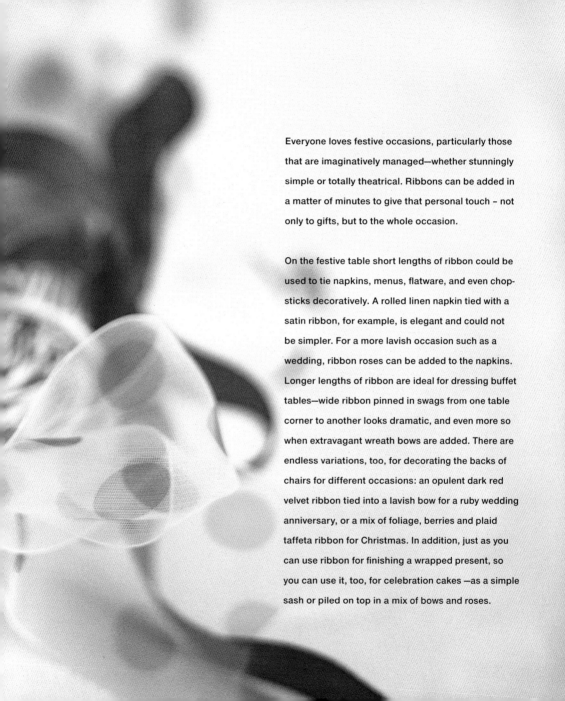

Everyone loves festive occasions, particularly those that are imaginatively managed—whether stunningly simple or totally theatrical. Ribbons can be added in a matter of minutes to give that personal touch – not only to gifts, but to the whole occasion.

On the festive table short lengths of ribbon could be used to tie napkins, menus, flatware, and even chopsticks decoratively. A rolled linen napkin tied with a satin ribbon, for example, is elegant and could not be simpler. For a more lavish occasion such as a wedding, ribbon roses can be added to the napkins. Longer lengths of ribbon are ideal for dressing buffet tables—wide ribbon pinned in swags from one table corner to another looks dramatic, and even more so when extravagant wreath bows are added. There are endless variations, too, for decorating the backs of chairs for different occasions: an opulent dark red velvet ribbon tied into a lavish bow for a ruby wedding anniversary, or a mix of foliage, berries and plaid taffeta ribbon for Christmas. In addition, just as you can use ribbon for finishing a wrapped present, so you can use it, too, for celebration cakes —as a simple sash or piled on top in a mix of bows and roses.

left A placecard is tied to the stem of a sweet pea with moiré taffeta ribbon and placed on a napkin.
above right Tiny bows in striped grosgrain complete these place cards.
below right Rolled menus are tied with organdy and placed in wine glasses.
far right An invitation is attached to a chair back by a narrow taffeta ribbon.

finishing touches

It is often the smallest details at a party table, whether it is for a large stylish wedding or an informal dinner for four, that make the most impact and thus turn it into a memorable occasion. However simple, such finishing touches add a sense of individual style.

The success of these details depends on using appropriate ribbons in a way that best complements the occasion. For Christmas and winter weddings, velvet ribbons in deep opulent colors and taffeta in traditional plaids are the perfect partners for white damask table linen, while for summer and outdoor occasions use organdy, which makes romantic-looking bows and shimmer in the light.

When choosing ribbons to finish your table, also consider, if any, the flowers. The ribbons should complement the flowers and the way in which they are presented, not only in color but also in texture. A navy and cream jacquard ribbon or pleated velvet, for example, would be too heavy to be used on the same table as an informal bowl of freshly picked sweet peas.

For the prettiest table settings, decorate menus and placecards with tiny bows secured with double-sided tape or a drop of glue. Punch holes in menus and invitations and thread with ribbon to hang from chair backs. The possibilities are as endless as the choice of ribbons.

left Pairs of chopsticks are elegantly tied with short lengths of cream satin and checked ribbon. The silky texture of the satin and the choice of color contrasts well with the matt black chopsticks. **right** For a buffet, satin ribbon in sophisticated shades of pale coffee, gray, and cream is used to tie flatware wrapped in thick white napkins.

Use ribbons instead of napkin rings to secure rolled napkins. Choose the ribbon to fit the occasion: try brightly striped and patterned ribbons for a summer party, satin and organdy for a wedding, or velvet for an extravagant dinner. Experiment with different ways of tying the napkin, as well as adding flowers and foliage. Another option is to tie ribbons around flatware, or decorate the handle of a wedding cake knife with a long ribbon of delicate organdy or silk, leaving the ends long so they drape and shimmer across the table.

top Ribbon tied around a rolled napkin makes an alternative napkin ring.
above A napkin folded into a square, rather than rolled, is gathered up and secured with a ribbon to match.

87

ribbon roses

The simplest ribbon roses are made from just one continuous strip of wire-edge ribbon, and there is no sewing involved, which makes them incredibly quick to make. A more elaborate double rose can be made using two different colored ribbons: two shades of pink, for example. Simply knot the two ribbons together at one end and proceed as for a single rose, ruffling and winding the two ribbons together. For each single rose you will need 1¼ yards of wire-edge ribbon.

one Tie a knot in the ribbon as close as possible to one end. At the opposite end, pull out the wire along one edge, so the ribbon starts to ruffle. **two** As you continue to pull the wire with one hand, gently tease the ribbon back toward the knot with the other hand. Pull until the length of ribbon is completely gathered. **three** Holding the knotted end in one hand, coil the gathered edge around the knot. Wind the remaining wire around the knot several times to secure. Gently tease out the ungathered edge of the ribbon so the rose looks more like a bloom than a tight bud. The excess wire can be trimmed or used to secure the flower to the napkin, as here.

An exquisite ribbon rose framed by
a floppy bow and tails in burgundy
organdy ribbon decorates the corner
of a table draped in crisp white linen.

right A rosette in checked wire-edge ribbon finished with a coordinating silky bow makes a wonderful corner decoration on a table set for a special occasion. The ends have been left extra long so they fall within the folds of the tablecloth.

far right Two lengths of ribbon, one diaphanous with a picot edge and the other satin, are looped and tied together in a simple bow and then pinned to the corner of a tablecloth for an incredibly easy yet effective decoration. The picot edge of the organdy ribbon picks up the eyelet detail of the white tablecloth.

tables and chairs

There are times when simply covering a table with a cloth is not quite effective enough for a special occasion, particularly when the table is to take center stage. A buffet table laden with food and flowers can look bare at the corners and sides because it is not surrounded by chairs. Similarly, a table intended for the wedding cake might need a little more decoration to emphasis its importance. For simplicity and speed, ribbons can simply be laid across a table like narrow runners and allowed to hang over the sides, or long lengths can be pinned from one corner to another in generous swags. Table corners look wonderful dressed with extravagant wreath bows or rosettes secured in place with long-tailed bows. Alternatively, place one tablecloth on top of another and gather up the top cloth at each corner with a bow to create opulent folds of fabric and reveal the contrasting cloth underneath.

left Lengths of brightly colored ribbon printed with white polka dots are casually placed across a table set for an alfresco meal. The varying lengths of ribbon and the two different widths add to the informality of the occasion.

below and right Add drama to a summer buffet table with ribbons in bright fluorescent colors. First pin a swag of shocking pink taffeta ribbon from one corner to another, choosing a woven rather than a wire-edge ribbon so that it will drape well across the cloth. Make single bows using the same ribbon and attach one to each corner, leaving the ends long. Make double bows from a contrasting ribbon with wire edges, which allows you to mold the loops of each bow into a full puffed-out shape. Pin these to each corner, on top of the single bows, to complete the decoration.

wreath bows

A wreath bow consists of two contrasting ribbons twisted into loops and then tied together to create

a wonderful froth of looping ribbon with long tails. You will need 2¾ yards of each ribbon, plus

6 inches of narrow ribbon or florist's wire.

one Set aside 20 inches of each ribbon. Place one

ribbon horizontally in front of you on a flat surface. Fold

the ribbon 7 inches from the right-hand edge to form the

first loop; return it to the center and twist it over. Fold the ribbon after another 7 inches, to form a second loop and return

the ribbon to the left, twisting it at the center as before. **two** Repeat this process until you have four loops on each side

of the center and the ends of the ribbon finish up on

opposite sides. Secure with a clothespin while you fold

and loop the contrasting ribbon. **three** Place one bow

on top of the other and tie them together in the center

with the narrow ribbon or wire. With one reserved ribbon

length on top of the other, place them under the bow. Tie

them in a single knot around the center of the bow to

hide the wire or narrow ribbon and form long tails. Fluff

up the bow, fanning out all the loops.

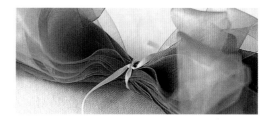

lift flap ▶

Just as party tables benefit from the addition of bows or a gentle swag of taffeta ribbon, so do chairs being used for special occasions. The decoration can be as simple as weaving ribbon through chair backs or, for a more elaborate effect, combining ribbon with seasonal flowers and tying them to the tops of chairs.

Choose a ribbon to complement the style of chair, taking note of its design, physical setting, and what it is made of. The top rung of a rustic wooden chair intended for an

informal party would look pretty decorated with an old-fashioned ribbon such as gingham or pale moss-green velvet. A curvaceous wrought-iron chair could be made to look even more romantic with a frothy bow in striped organdy, while a dark oak chair always looks good with traditional ribbons such as velvets, taffeta plaids, and jacquards in rich sumptuous colors. Lengths of ribbon used on the backs of chairs can be useful, too, besides being decorative—ideal for hanging small wreaths, tiny gift bags, or posies, for example.

left Wide creamy satin ribbon is woven through the slatted back of a wooden chair and then finished in a large floppy bow, ready for a wedding party.

above A checked ribbon woven with metallic thread is used to tie a small bundle of foliage and flowers to the back of a chair. The gold thread picks up the gold paint of the chair.

right In sharp contrast to the size of the hydrangea, a long length of narrow satin ribbon is used to secure the flower to the back of chair and then tied in a loose bow.

This cake is strikingly but very simply decorated with a sash made from two contrasting ribbons. A length of wide pleated orange taffeta is wrapped around the cake and topped with a narrower black and white ribbon with a picot edge.

celebration cakes

left A pink wire-edge ribbon has been passed beneath an iced cake and tied in a bow on top. A single bow in a contrasting color is added for an extravagant finish.

below left An exquisite floral braided ribbon is arranged in swags around an iced cake and pinned in position. Small grosgrain bows in matching vibrant blue with red edging have been added to the top of the swags.

below For a sophisticated centerpiece, a cake is dressed with a sash of silk and topped with a ribbon rose and bow.

special presentation

As with most of the ideas in this book, the decorating of gifts or other items with ribbon requires no special skills or tools—just a little care, thought, and imagination. However simply applied, ribbon can transform a quite ordinary object into something special. The ribbon should enhance the item it is decorating, not smother it. A glass bowl, for example, would look far more dramatic adorned with a single beautiful satin bow than with a highly patterned ribbon tied in a complicated bow.

The different colors and textures of ribbon and the manner in which it is applied determines the different effects possible. A gift wrapped in white tissue paper, tied with a shimmering pastel-colored organdy and finished in a bow with long trailing ends, has a soft feminine look.

above left Old-fashioned tiny candy boxes made from thin white cardboard are closed with silky ribbon cord and displayed on a glass cake stand.

below left Cones overflowing with Easter treats are decorated with crisscrossed remnants of silk ribbon topped with a bow of narrow organdy ribbon.

right Duck's eggs for an Easter display are trimmed with an assortment of narrow ribbons. It is best to secure the ribbon at one end of each egg first by gluing it in position before tying the ribbon into a bow at the other end.

far left A large present wrapped in handmade Japanese paper is decorated with different but complementary diaphanous ribbons – a narrow organdy ribbon placed over a wider ribbon of satin-edge georgette.

left Homemade cookies have been stacked into piles, then wrapped in clear cellophane and secured with a rubber band. They are decorated with ribbon tied into a simple bow only at the top, or wrapped around the whole gift and finished with a bow.

The same gift would look quite different, however, if it was decorated with a chic navy grosgrain ribbon, knotted or tied in a small neat bow.

When choosing ribbon, consider the size of the item since you do not want to swamp it with too much ribbon; similarly, too narrow a ribbon on a large object will look out of proportion and stingy. Other factors to consider are the "feel" you wish to convey. For a traditional Christmas look, the obvious ribbons are metallics in gold, taffeta in red and green plaids, and deep, richly colored velvets; while for a more flamboyant look, wire-edge ribbons in vibrant turquoises and purples are more appropriate.

The color and texture of the wrapped gift or the surface of the object to be decorated should also be considered. For a contrast of textures, team a silky satin ribbon with a heavily textured handmade paper, or a picot-edge organdy with a shiny cellophane wrap. Or experiment with contrasts of color and pattern: a fine jacquard ribbon wrapped around a bowl with cracked glazing, or a duck's egg trimmed with a georgette ribbon.

Using two different ribbons together offers other possibilities. You could try pairing up plain and patterned ribbons of the same or of differing widths for various effects.

left The top of a wooden bucket is decorated with a gingham swag and neat bows in a contrasting ribbon before being used to hold napkins at a buffet party.

Not all presents need be hidden in wrapping paper. These Japanese bowls, some filled with candy, are simply tied with different ribbons—a picot- and satin-edge sheer, a picot-edge grosgrain, and a checked satin.

For example, team a pale blue cotton tape with a blue and white gingham, or perhaps a black silk with a black and yellow polka dot.

In addition to presents, containers such as baskets, vases, and cake stands all benefit from a decoration of ribbon. It might be as simple a trick as tying a taffeta bow to the handle of a pewter jug, weaving a grosgrain ribbon around the top of a basket, or trimming the rim of a wooden bowl with small bows. If the decoration is only temporary, secure the ribbon with double-sided tape or, for permanence, use dabs of strong multipurpose glue. The thing to remember is not to overdo the decoration. Always resist the temptation of using too much ribbon, however beautiful it might be.

left A stack of wrapped soap is tied together and then finished with a chic matching pleated bow.
right Small bottles of bath oil are wrapped in lilac organza and finished with two different ribbons combined together into one simple bow.

festive decorations

A bare room or an unadorned Christmas tree can be quickly transformed with just a few lengths of colorful ribbon. Use short lengths, perhaps remnants from another ribbon project or left over from gift wrapping, to decorate plain Christmas-tree balls. Carefully remove each ball's metal neck and wire loop before decorating. Secure the lengths of ribbon at the base and around the neck of the ball with either strong glue or, if only temporary, with double-sided tape. When the neck piece is replaced, it should cover the ribbon ends. For elegant simplicity all the balls could be decorated with just one type of ribbon—a red ball trimmed with plaid or metallic grosgrain ribbon, for example—or you might prefer a coordinated mixture: polka dots, checks, and stripes in black and white around silver balls.

left These Christmas-tree balls are decorated with ribbon and hung as a group, then crowned with a length of striped ribbon folded into floppy loops. Decorating plain balls in this way is an excellent way of using up small pieces of exquisite ribbon you cannot bear to throw away.

right Simple white candles look sophisticated when tied into a pile with two contrasting ribbons – a wide diaphanous organdy is offset by a narrower ribbon of turquoise grosgrain edged in lime green. The ends of the latter have been deliberately left long to trail over the table.

Besides enhancing balls, you can use ribbon to revamp old tree decorations or create new ones from unusual odds and ends, making good use of color and texture. Alternatively, decorate your Christmas tree with just bows: single and double bows in dark-colored satin, or a mix of gold wire mesh and metallic ribbons. Crown the tree with one spectacular bow to finish.

far left A sumptuous satin bow decorates a candle holder.

left Glass drops, remnants of a broken chandelier, are tied with ribbons of various widths to make tree decorations.

above As an alternative to the traditional Christmas tree, a branch is hung with starfish on lengths of pale ribbon.

Ribbons to decorate the home work best when used boldly and simply. Tie bows to chandeliers, leaving the ends long to flutter gently and shimmer in the light. Add trailing bows to the base of candlesticks and vases. Attach bows to the tops of mirrors and pictures and, on an even larger scale, decorate fireplaces, tables, staircases, and doors with swathes of ribbon.

above and right A mantelpiece, hung with pleated orange taffeta ribbon and picture bows in checked ribbon, is the focal point for a festive room. The taffeta is twisted as it is arranged in loops and held in position with double-sided tape. The picture bows can be taped or pinned on top.

ribbon wreaths

left and far left A twig wreath has been lightly sprayed with white paint and decorated with six bows in a sheer ribbon, on top of which are smaller contrasting bows in narrow gingham and taffeta edged with satin.

overleaf left, clockwise from top left A wreath base covered with wide metallic ribbon and decorated with gold bows makes an alternative to the traditional Christmas wreath of berries and foliage.

A length of pleated wire-edge ribbon forms a scalloped wreath when it is pinched at regular intervals and tied to a circular wire frame with contrasting ribbon.

A door knob is decorated with a wreath hung from a loop of red and cream checked taffeta ribbon.

A wedding wreath is covered with ribbon roses and simple bows.

overleaf, right In keeping with its delicate quality, this wreath of dried leaves has been hung by a diaphanous satin-edge ribbon.

ribbons and flowers

Ribbons are particularly effective when used with flowers. A length of ribbon casually tied into a simple bow is all that is required to turn a simple bunch of garden flowers into something special. A tiny posy of violets needs no more than a plush velvet ribbon to become exquisite, while a mix of cow parsley, sweet peas, and other summer flowers is delightful when tied with a froth of shimmering organdy. Different effects can be achieved, according to the type of ribbon used and the way in which it is applied. A bouquet of pale-colored roses bound and finished with a thick satin ribbon will look luxurious and suitable for a wedding, while the same flowers tied with a pretty gingham bow will look more relaxed and informal.

Ribbons may also be used to decorate vases, pitchers, or pots of flowers, and work well with single flowers and buds to produce pretty boutonnieres.

posies

far left A bunch of old-fashioned columbine is held with two different but complementary ribbons tied in a simple bow.

above left A tiny posy of sweetly scented lily-of-the-valley is tied with a frothing bow of almost translucent ribbon decorated with tiny dots.

below left Lilac and sweet peas are decorated with a wide lilac velvet ribbon.

above The choice of a velvet ribbon for this exquisite posy has been dictated by the velvety petals and colors of the violas.

ribbon-wrapped bouquet

Wrapping the stems of a bouquet with ribbon is done for both

decorative and practical reasons, particularly for a wedding

bouquet that will probably be held for a long time. To bind a small

bouquet, you will need 1¼ yards of 1 inch wide satin ribbon, plus

florist's wire or string, and tape or multipurpose glue.

one Using string, florist's wire, or narrow ribbon, tie the flower stems together

at both ends. Trim all the stem ends to the same length. Cut the length of satin

ribbon in half. Take one length and wrap one end at an angle around the base of the stems as shown. Bring the ribbon

around, close to the cut stem ends and over the ribbon end to secure it in position.

two Continue to wrap the ribbon around the stems, keeping the ribbon taut and

making sure each overlap is evenly spaced

and at the same angle. When the stems are

completely covered, cut the excess ribbon and

secure the end of the wrapped ribbon with

either tape or a drop of glue. **three** Place the second length of ribbon under

the stems at the end of the wrapped ribbon. Tie a simple bow over the top of

the wrapped ribbon to help secure it and to finish off the bouquet.

l i f t   f l a p ▶

below This boutonniere of white flowers and ivy was purchased from a florist, but it has been given a personal touch by the addition of a simple bow of chic black and white polka-dot satin ribbon.

far right, top The wired stem of this boutonniere has been stylishly bound in a striped satin ribbon, using the same technique as for binding the stems of a bouquet.

far right, center A satin-edge taffeta ribbon has been carefully selected to pick out the colored markings on the orchid and is tied in a bow just below the petals.

far right, below Highlighting the contrast in textures, a narrow cream-colored grosgrain ribbon with a picot edge is teamed with a smooth camellia blossom and knotted around the stem instead of being tied in a bow.

A wide wire-edge ribbon is gathered
along one edge, as for making a rosette
bow (see page 150), and then wound
around the top of the stems of a simple
bouquet to frame the flower heads. The
rich color of the flowers is intensified
here by the use of a purple ribbon.

The stripes within this satin organdy ribbon make a feature of the flower stems, while the delicacy of both the ribbon's color and its texture echoes that of the flowers in the bouquet.

boutonnieres

Creating attractive boutonnieres or corsages for lapels offers enormous scope and fun for combining flowers, foliage, and ribbons for a variety of different effects.

Wedding favorites can be presented in completely original ways: for example, a classic red rose finished with black and white gingham ribbon, or ivy paired with a striped silk. The choice of flower or foliage, and the way in which it is decorated, should reflect the feel of the occasion. For a formal wedding, a rose or tulip bud beautifully dressed with satin ribbon is suitable, while a blue delphinium finished with a blue and white checked bow is perfect for a summer country wedding, and a burnt orange dahlia tied with ruby red grosgrain is flamboyant. The effect is all in the detail, however simple it is.

Besides suiting the style of the wedding, boutonnieres can be an important part of an outfit. For example, the groom's boutonniere should enhance as well as coordinate with part of his attire, such as his tie or vest. With this in mind, do not mix pattern with pattern. A spray of pretty foliage tied with floral jacquard ribbon woven in greens, yellows, and oranges looks far better with a plain mustard-colored vest than with a brocade one or with a checked tie. Instead, team these with a plain solid ribbon that picks up one of the colors in the pattern and perhaps even match the fabric used, pairing a silk ribbon with a silk tie, for example.

above Boutonnieres do not necessarily have to consist of a traditional flower, such as a rose or a carnation, formally paired with a shiny satin ribbon. Try using unusual flowers and distinctive foliage instead. For this more casual look, tie a narrow picot-edge ribbon around a small sprig of foliage in a classic shoelace style bow, or match the distinctive small lime green flowers of lady's mantle with a finely striped silk ribbon.

right A bright orange gerbera appears even more flamboyant when tied with a length of turquoise grosgrain ribbon edged with lime green. This softer-textured grosgrain can be tied in a bow, unlike some of the stiffer versions.

far right Experiment with ribbon width, size of bow, and color when creating boutonnieres. Black and white gingham is effective here with fresh green colors.

left Cream grosgrain ribbon with a picot edge is used to decorate a galvanized bucket with stripes, making it a perfect table centerpiece.

below The handle of an old enamel water pitcher of flowers is decorated with a diaphanous pale blue ribbon tied in a large floppy bow.

vases and flowerpots

Bouquets and pots of flowers presented as gifts are often decorated with a bow, and after they are unwrapped it is a shame not to make the most of the ribbon. Use it by tying it casually into a loose bow around the vase neck or onto the handle. Alternatively, using a good multipurpose glue, attach stripes of ribbon on the surface of a container to make a decorative grid or striped pattern. Thicker ribbons such as grosgrains and woven jacquards are particularly suited for this type of decoration, adding not only color and pattern, but also an attractive texture.

Ribbon can also be used to hang glass jars filled with flowers. Choose a jar with a neck and a slight lip around the top. Knot one length of ribbon tightly around the neck and tie the ends in a bow. With a second length of ribbon, make a handle by which to hang the jar.

above left A striped silk bow trims a potted plant.
above right This flower-filled glass jar is hung like a lantern by a length of plain ribbon and decoratively finished with a patterned jacquard ribbon tied in a bow.

types of ribbon

There is an astonishing choice of ribbon color, texture, pattern, and width—varying from ¹⁄₁₆ inch to 6 inches—and each ribbon type has its most appropriate uses. For example, a hard-wearing washable and colorfast ribbon should be used if it is to be subjected to wear and tear, while more delicate ribbons are better suited for decorative purposes. The following ribbons are those most used in this book.

Satin and taffeta Satin ribbons are available as either single face (shiny on one side and matte on the other) or double face (shiny on both sides). They are available in single colors as well as patterns and may be finished with a delicate picot edge. Taffeta, in contrast to satin, is nearly always matte and the same on both sides. It comes in solid colors, traditional plaids, checks, and stripes. Ombré taffeta is color-shaded from one edge to the other, and moiré taffeta shimmers with a watermark. Both satin and taffeta ribbons are available with wire edges and with metallic trimmed edges.

Sheer Sheer ribbons, which include organdy and georgette, are made from very finely woven yarns so are light and delicate and appear almost translucent. Organdy is often "shot"—an effect produced by weaving the ribbon from two contrasting colors so it changes color or appearance according to the way the light falls on it. Georgettes have a slightly matte appearance because of their crepe texture. Sheer ribbons are often manufactured with a thicker woven or wire edge, which helps to give the fabric stability. They may be plain or printed with delicate floral patterns, appliquéd or embroidered, or incorporate a metallic thread. Sheer ribbons drape well and make the most frothy and romantic bows, particularly wreath bows (see page 98).

Jacquard These ribbons are woven, rather than printed, with patterns ranging from the simplest of images to highly elaborate designs involving many colors. The weaving adds texture and creates a right and a wrong side so the ribbon is best used in a simple way where the patterns can be seen and appreciated fully.

Grosgrain These ribbons have a distinctive crosswise rib and are stronger and thicker to handle than most of the other ribbons. Grosgrain was traditionally used by milliners to decorate hats. The ribbon is available in solid colors, appliquéd, patterned —often striped—pleated, and with picot edges.

Velvet This classic ribbon is woven with a distinctive plush pile, usually on one side only. For this reason it looks best when used in very simple ways. Velvet ribbon is available in various widths and can be found in single colors, as well as with printed or flocked patterns, pleated, and with a wire edge. The fabric, particularly fine silk velvets, should be treated with care as the pile can be easily crushed from repeated tying and knotting. Dressmaking pins will also mark velvet, so try to keep their use to a minimum.

Braided ribbon Whereas most ribbons are woven as narrow strips of fabric with two straight selvage edges, braided ribbons—which are often very narrow and delicate—are woven with shaped edges or are woven into shapes and intricate patterns. They range in complexity from traditional cotton rickrack to exquisite three-dimensional rosebuds and leaves strung together like daisy chains. Braided ribbons are nearly all washable, making them particularly suitable for edging table and bed linen and for decorating clothing and home furnishings.

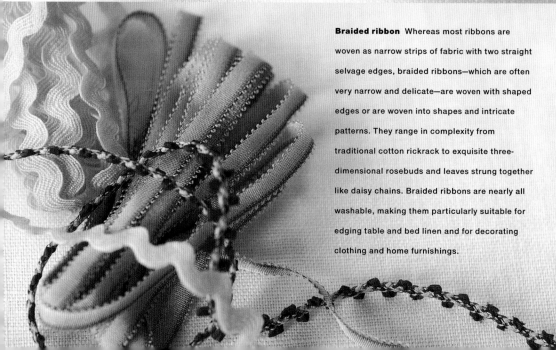

Metallics These ribbons are made from metallic threads, either used alone or combined with other fibers. They may also be printed with metallic motifs, which makes them a popular choice for festive occasions.

Wire-edge ribbons Most fabric ribbons are available with wire edges—a fine flexible wire woven along both edges—which helps the ribbon hold its shape when made into a bow, or which may be pulled to gather the ribbon for a ruffled effect. Most wire-edge ribbons cannot be washed. The wire can easily be removed if a "normal" ribbon is required.

Pleated and ruffled Most ribbon textures are available not only as flat fabric strips, but also come ready pleated, ruched, or ruffled. These techniques may have been worked over the whole ribbon, for example, a pleated taffeta or velvet, or along just one or both edges, as with a ruffle-edge satin or a ruched gingham. Such ribbons are not suitable for tying into elaborate bows, but are best used simply; they are ideal for edging home furnishings: pillows, lampshades, and curtains.

single bow

This is the simplest bow of all and suitable for any type of ribbon. There is no twisting or complicated

looping, so it is particularly suitable for ribbon with a right and wrong side, such as jacquard or

velvet, as well as heavier ribbon like grosgrain,

which is less versatile and difficult to knot well.

You will need 20 inches of ribbon, plus a short

length of narrow ribbon or florist's wire.

one Lay the ribbon horizontally on a flat surface in front

of you. Overlap the two ends of the ribbon as shown.

two Pinch the ribbon together in the center, gathering

up the fabric. **three** Tie the pinched center with the

narrow ribbon or florist's wire, knotting it at the back of

the bow. Do not cut the excess ribbon or wire yet in case

it is needed to secure the bow to something. Puff out the

bow loops and twist the ends to point downward. If you

have not already done so, cut the ends of the ribbon

diagonally or in an inverted V shape (see page 151).

double bow

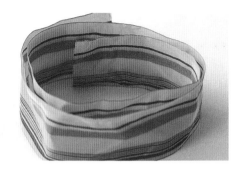

You will need about 1¾ yards of ribbon—allow more for a very wide ribbon—plus a short length of narrow ribbon or florist's wire.

one Cut off a 20 inch length of ribbon and put to one side. On a flat surface arrange the remaining ribbon in a coil with both ends of ribbon finishing opposite each other at roughly the same point, but slightly overlapping the center. Flatten the coil, keeping the ribbon ends near the center with the loops for the bow at each side. **two** Pinch the center of the flattened coil and tie it either with narrow ribbon or florist's wire. Secure tightly at the back of the bow.

three To make the ends, slide the reserved ribbon length under the bow and tie it around the center, knotting it at the back. Fan out the bow loops and cut the ends diagonally or in an inverted V shape (see page 151).

picture bow

Use one single ribbon or two contrasting ones.

You will need about 1¼ yards of ribbon, plus

6 inches of narrow ribbon or florist's wire.

one   Set aside a 16 inch length of the ribbon and

arrange the remainder to make four loops as shown. Flat-

ten, making sure the ends of the ribbon are in a central

position but slightly overlapping the center, with two loops arranged on each side.   **two**   Fold the reserved ribbon

length in half and lay it under the flattened loops to make a cross, with the three loops of equal length. Place the narrow

ribbon or wire under the vertical loop; bring both ends to the front to cross over in the center.   **three**   Take the ends to

the back. Pull tightly to gather up the center of the bow and knot to secure the loops and tails. Trim the loose ends.

four   Gently puff out the bow and tails; cut the ends in an inverted V (see page 151) if you have not already done so.

pleated bow

This simple bow is ideal for ribbons that are difficult to knot. You will need 22 inches of 1½ inches wide ribbon, and 4 inches of a 1 inch wide contrasting ribbon.

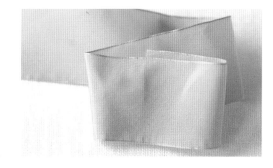

one Place the longer length of ribbon horizontally on a flat surface in front of you. Turn under 1½ inches at the right-hand edge to form the first loop. Fold the ribbon again after 3 inches to form a second loop, returning the ribbon to the right, behind the first loop. **two** Repeat this folding and looping, making the next two loops slightly wider apart than the first two and the final two loops even more so, to produce three sets of loops of increasing width—the shortest at the front. The end of the ribbon should finish in a central position in line with the beginning.

three Secure the pleated ribbon with a staple in the center. To finish the bow, wrap the shorter length of ribbon around the center to cover the staple and secure at the back with either a dab of multipurpose glue or double-sided tape. Gently puff out the loops, if desired.

rosette bow

You will need 2½ yards of a single wire-edge ribbon, or use contrasting colors or fabrics.

one Cut a 24 inch length of the wire-edge ribbon and lay it on a flat surface. Take one corner and pull out ⅜ inch

of wire from the ribbon edge. Bend this end of wire back along itself to secure it. Take the end of the wire on the

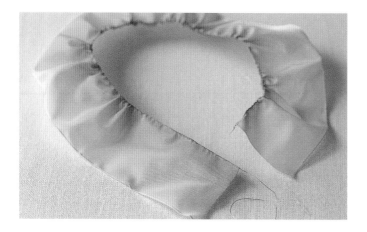

corresponding edge at the other end of the ribbon, and pull it out gently so the ribbon starts to ruffle and curl into a horseshoe shape.

two As you continue to pull the wire out with one hand, gently tease the ruffles back toward the other

end with your other hand. Keep pulling the wire until the length of ribbon is completely gathered. Cut the excess

wire, leaving a 1 inch end to bend back along itself, as before, to secure the gathers. Fold under the last ⅜ inch

of the ribbon to hide the raw edge. Arrange the gathered

ribbon into a circle, overlapping the two ends slightly and

making sure the neat turned-under edge is on top. Using

a needle, with thread chosen to match the ribbon, join

the ends together with a few stitches to make a circle.

three Cut 20 inches of ribbon and repeat as for the first length of ribbon to make a slightly smaller gathered circle.

Make a third circle using 16 inches of ribbon. To assemble the bow, place the three gathered circles on top of each

other, the largest at the bottom and the smallest on top. **four** Place the circles on the object or surface you wish

to decorate. Place the
center of the remaining
length of ribbon in the
middle of the circles. Pin

it to the object or surface beneath, or stick it using a drop

of multipurpose glue—this will hold the circles in place.

five Fold each tail end in half; cut at an angle to make a

perfectly symmetrical inverted V at each end. **six** Tie the

loose ends into a bow and pull the tails downward.

acknowledgments

This book would not have been possible without the help and commitment of the following people. A very big thank you to Annabelle Lewis and everyone at her wonderful shop, VV Rouleaux, for all their enthusiasm and enormous help. I'd also like to thank Suki Dhanda, Claudia Dulak, and Rosalind Fairman. I am indebted to Fiona Lindsay, my agent, for her guidance and encouragement, and to Jacqui Small who invited me to do this book. I'd also like to give a big thank you to everyone at Ryland Peters and Small, in particular Sally Powell who made sense of all the pictures and designed such a wonderful looking book, and Jo Lethaby who so calmly brought order to the text.

In particular I wish to thank Sandra Lane who, in spite of the imminent arrival of Billy, took as always the most beautiful pictures. This book would not have been the same without her. Finally, a very special thank you to Charles, who is always a constant support and inspiration to me. **This book is dedicated to the "flower girls"—Jenny, Gilly, and Kath with love.**

suppliers

Bell'occhio
8 Brady Street
San Francisco, CA 94103
415-864-4048
Vintage ribbons

Britex Fabrics
146 Geary Street
San Francisco, CA 94108
415-392-2910
Ribbons and trimmings

Conso Products
P. O. Box 326
Union, SC 29379
800-845-2431
Distributors of decorative
trims, cordings, ropings,
tassels, and fringes

Hollywood Trims
P. O. Box 5028
Spartanburg, SC 29304
Manufacturers and
distributors of metallic trims,
cordings, and tassels

Hyman Hendler & Sons
67 West 38th Street
New York, NY 10018
212-840-8393
Fabulous selection of ribbons

Lion Brand Ribbon
(Affiliate of C. M. Offray & Son)
Route 24
P. O. Box 601
Chester, NJ 07930
Makers of craft and speciality
ribbons of all sorts

M & J Trimmings Co.
1008 Sixth Avenue
New York, NY 10018
212-391-9072
A wide range of trimmings

M. P. R. Associates, Inc.
P. O. Box 7343
High Point, NC 27264
800-454-3331
Nontraditional ribbons includ-
ing paper lace, corrugated
paper ribbons, wired and plain
paper and metallic ribbons,
paper rafia, and paper twist

Maxwell • Wellington
811 West Evergreen, Suite 306
Chicago, IL 60622
312-943-2866

Fax: 312-943-9194
Ribbons of paper, velvets and
metallics in a variety of widths,
available with or without wires
or as handmade bows.

Midori Inc.
3827 Stone Way North
Seatlle, WA98103
Call 800-659-3049 for retail
information

Tinsel Trading Co.
47 West 38th Street
New York, NY 10018
212-730-1030
Unique collection of vintage to
contemporary trims, tassels,
flowers, fringes, buttons,
cords, and military trims